THE
BOXFORD MOSAIC
A Unique Survivor from the Roman Age

(DS)

Anthony Beeson, Matt Nichol & Joy Appleton

COUNTRYSIDE BOOKS
NEWBURY BERKSHIRE

First published 2019
© 2019 Countryside Books

COUNTRYSIDE BOOKS
3 Catherine Road
Newbury, Berkshire

To view our complete range of books please visit us at
www.countrysidebooks.co.uk

ISBN 978 1 84674 392 4

Thanks to the following for supplying the photographs:
Nicholas Battle (NB), Anthony Beeson (AB), Lyons Sleeman Hoare, Architects (LSH),
Chris Forsey (CF), Cotswold Archaeology (CA), Richard Miller (RM),
Matt Nichol (MN), David Shepherd (DS)

All materials used in the manufacture of this book carry FSC certification

Produced by The Letterworks Ltd., Reading
Designed and Typeset by KT Designs, St Helens
Printed by Holywell Press, Oxford

CONTENTS

INTRODUCTION
By Joy Appleton

How was this amazing discovery of the Boxford Mosaic at Mud Hole found? We have to go back more than ten years to find out.

By 2007, the demographics of the village of Boxford, West Berkshire, had changed considerably. In order to understand the wishes of residents, a survey was commissioned, supported by West Berkshire Council with a grant from the National Lottery Awards for All fund. There was a remarkably high return rate of 80%. From this a Parish Plan was drawn up, incorporating all the results. Support for history-related elements – such as preserving the history of the parish, writing a history book and supporting a museum – received high scores, not surprising really since many newcomers knew little of the area, certainly little before World War II.

The Boxford History Project (BHP) was set up in 2008 – its first task was to write a simple history of the parish, since an earlier history *Boxford Barleycorn* written by Elsie Huntley had gone out of print. The book *Boxora to Boxford* came out two years later after much research.

One mystery remained despite the research work – the team could track Stone Age, Bronze Age, Iron Age and Saxons in the parish but little was known about the Romans except for some Roman pottery and one villa marked on old maps. The team deduced that Romans *must* have lived in Boxford. Boxford was about halfway between Cirencester and Silchester, it was served by Ermin Street, the Roman equivalent of the M4, it had a wonderfully clear chalk river, the River Lambourn, for a water supply and for fishing, and it was surrounded by highly productive land, with wild boar and deer roaming its woodland – it was idyllic.

Researcher Sue Downes followed up a lead from one of the older members of the community, Eileen Kemp, who had found Roman tile many years before. Sue found more and when Berkshire Archaeological Research Group (BARG) members visited Boxford to see the recently revealed Saxon window in the church, they took the opportunity to look at the site and thought it was worth progressing. There was also mention of a building being found in 1871 during the digging of a field land drain, which assisted with working out the potential location of the Mud Hole site.

So that was the beginning of the archaeological investigations, which begun in 2012 and continued each year to 2017 into the three Roman sites in Boxford: a villa at Hoar Hill, a farmstead at Wyfield and a modest villa at Mud Hole. The BHP led the projects, raised funds, provided manpower and organised the logistics. BARG provided archaeological expertise but each time excavations took place, Matt Nichol from Cotswold Archaeology (CA) was on hand to supervise the excavations. This was necessary for although volunteers were becoming more proficient as time went on, the sites were so important that a professional approach was necessary to do them justice. The volunteers understood and appreciated that they were working to a professional standard.

In August 2017, the last project in a three-year Heritage Lottery-funded series was the villa building at Mud Hole near the parish boundary of Boxford and Winterbourne. During the first week the site lived up to its name – a pond appeared outside the marquee, complete with ducks!

However, by the time the JCB arrived on site, it was dry and the topsoil could be cleared off the barn. Matt Nichol, acting as banksman, and JCB driver Scudd Giles then started work on the first of the trenches on what was thought to be the villa building. A shout came up from Matt and the JCB

stopped. Just below the surface, a band of large red tesserae could be seen. This was the border of the mosaic. The rest, as they say, is history. Due to the tight time constraints of farming, only a third of the mosaic was uncovered in 2017. Although damaged in part, it was highly figurative and described by experts at the time as being the most important mosaic find in Britain in the last fifty years.

It took most of 2018 and the beginning of 2019 for the BHP to raise enough funds from multiple donors to enable the project to uncover the whole mosaic. The Good Exchange provided a crowdfunding platform, which added valuable funds to the coffers.

However, volunteers were more than forthcoming! Applications rolled in from over 100 with a goodly number

Boxford Mosaic when partly uncovered in 2017. (RM)

Day 1 for the diggers in 2019. (DS)

from Boxford and the immediate area, supplemented by individual members of BARG and other archaeological groups. One application was from an amateur archaeologist from Ohio with expertise in the pre-history of the American Midwest whose lifelong dream was to excavate a Roman site. Applications outstripped places and Jenny Hayward came in to organise the roster.

Three of the volunteers were expert photographers and have made a wonderful record of the excavations – some of their photos can be seen on the following pages. Students who had joined earlier projects at aged sixteen returned once again, now with degrees in Archaeology, History or Classics.

However we should not forget all those who came from a wide range of backgrounds in the community to lend their expertise and support, some even used their annual leave to take part.

The three mattockeers – Jim Calow, Gary and Jack Burton. (CF)

Anthony Beeson on Open Day. (DS)

Matt, Sam and Agata from Cotswold Archaeology. (RM)

A section showing the foundation of the mosaic. The tesserae were laid and grouted on a thin layer of lime bonding cement over a bed of ginger coloured sand on top of compacted chalk and clay. (AB)

Mention must be made of Anthony Beeson, *iconographer extraordinaire*, who arrived for the second week of the dig and virtually lived on the mosaic until it was reburied. As various scenes on the mosaic were uncovered, those watching found his expert interpretation of the mosaic stories both illuminating and entertaining.

The Cotswold Archaeology team on site was led by Matt Nichol with help from Sam Wilson and Agata Kowalska. Duncan Coe was their Project Director. Agata first came as a volunteer in 2015 and 2016, and by 2017 was working as a trainee archaeologist with Cotswold Archaeology. She is now a fully-fledged archaeologist and it was a pleasure to see her on site.

The project in August 2019 was blessed with dry weather – so Mud Hole did *not* live up to its name. Indeed it was incredibly hot in the first week and particularly over the Bank Holiday weekend. However, the project started for the BHP team on Saturday 17th August with the erection of two marquees, one for cover in the event of bad weather and the other for finds processing, and a gazebo. Gary Burton erected his tent, used every year since Wyfield excavations, for tool storage. Another stalwart, Jim Callow, brought in scaffold planks and tarpaulins to cover the mosaic if necessary. On Monday 19th August, Matt Nichol quickly set up the trench lines and the JCB driver, Scudd Giles, began carefully removing the topsoil. Meanwhile, the BHP team brought in tables and chairs and a lot of additional

Opposite: Matt washing tesserae and revealing the colour and detail for the first time. (DS)

equipment. This would have been problematic had it not been for the sterling efforts of Nick Battle and his white van. The water supply was laid and connected thanks to the owners of the adjacent property; the loos were delivered and the security system set up.

So the site was open for volunteers on Tuesday 20th. The first week's work was seriously hard with mattocks being used most of the time for the removal of the flint and stone debris from the wall and roof collapses of the Roman villa. However, at the end of week one everyone was rewarded by the sight of the first of four telamones on the north-western corner of the mosaic in an area previously unseen. The relief of seeing the undamaged figure was palpable. There was a gasp from the group watching as Matt sponged the tesserae and the outline of the figure came to life.

Week two was something of a blur as more mosaic was uncovered and the mythical stories changed almost daily to begin with as Anthony teased out the pictures in the mosaic. The BBC had attempted coverage of the 2017 story of the mosaic's discovery but had arrived too late, after it had been reburied. This time, they wanted to be part of the action. South Today sent out a reporter and cameraman on the second Wednesday and agreed to wait until Friday, the day before the Open Day, before they screened it. Radio Berkshire's three-hour Bill Buckley show came live from the site that Friday and he was able to interview many of the local volunteers as well as Matt and Anthony.

This BBC coverage no doubt explains the tremendous response to the single, free Open Day on Saturday 31st

The team at work. (DS)

Cleaning the mosaic with a toothbrush. (RM)

August when around 3,000 people turned up in the field. Thankfully, BHP members and some of the volunteers worked wonders in dealing with the 1,200 cars that arrived. Boxford and Winterbourne villages were at a standstill.

All hands covered the explanation of the mosaic and the villa building to the expectant crowds. Anthony and Matt in Trench 2, Sam in Trench 1, the room adjacent to the mosaic. Alice Jones, one of our volunteers in 2016, covered the explanation of the many Greek myths on the mosaic whilst Anthony had a break. Many in the crowd came away and voiced their delight in what they had seen and the quality of explanations given. Many visitors queued to see the finds in one of the marquees. Such was the general air of approbation and generosity that the donation buckets were filled to overflowing and £4,500 was raised on that one day! The money will be used to fund the conservation of the objects found during the dig.

After the excitement of the Open Day, the following week was relatively quiet with Matt and the team meticulously recording the villa building and the mosaic before it was reburied. Sponsors and owners came to view the mosaic at a special event and were astonished that a community group had succeeded in achieving such an impressive project in ten days. They were also impressed by the erudition of the mosaic's caretaker, Anthony! And so the mosaic went to bed again, covered by a duvet of nearly four tons of sieved soil by three volunteers before Scudd and the JCB finished the job by backfilling and turning the area back into an agricultural field.

Joy being interviewed by BBC South Today. (DS)

Open Day – over 3,000 people came to see the mosaic. (DS)

Open Day. Matt and Anthony. (DS)

Community volunteers have again been the mainstay of this project. It has been the policy of allowing anyone interested to take part, in whatever way they were able. Not everyone can wield a mattock and some jobs are a bit mundane but are genuinely important like cleaning and recording finds. David and Prue Willison plus Jenny and John Hayward together with Nick Battle were with us every day to do the running around as well as finds processing.

Everyone on site worked really hard no matter what their role and there was a really good atmosphere.

Although oversubscribed several times by volunteers this year, Jenny Hayward ensured that everyone had a place. No one was turned away. The volunteers have done an incredible job in not only uncovering this unique mosaic but by excavating the adjacent room, they added to our understanding of the villa building as a whole. And all this in just ten days of excavation – absolutely extra-ordinary and amazing!

It only remains for me to say a very humble thank you to the landowners for their interest and permission, the sponsors listed below and the many hundreds who used The Good Exchange crowdfunding platform to support

The unglamorous but essential processing of finds. (DS)

Opposite: The team, 2019. (MN)

this project. Without this level of generosity, the project would never have got off the ground.

On a personal note, I would like to take this opportunity to thank the BHP trustees and the membership for their hard work over a long period to achieve this project … and for keeping me on the straight and narrow!

Joy Appleton

Sponsors

The Headley Trust

The Adrian Swire Charitable Trust

The Ardeola Charitable Trust

The North Wessex Downs Landscape SDF

The Mick Aston Fund – Council of British Archaeology

Greenham Common Trust

Englefield Charitable Trust

The Good Exchange

Newbury Building Society

ASPROM – The Association for the Study and Preservation of Roman Mosaics

There were many other private and generous donations

Boxford History Project Trustees

THE HISTORY OF THE VILLA:
DISCOVERY OF A ROMAN MASTERPIECE
By Matt Nichol

That View...

I had been engaged to undertake archaeological excavations in 2017 and recently in 2019 at the Mud Hole villa site, just outside the picturesque village of Boxford in West Berkshire. We were working on behalf of the Boxford History Project, and I became fascinated by the positioning of the villa. It was situated in what appeared at first glance to be just a regular field – yet to me that field felt like it had an almost amphitheatre or stage-like quality to it. Roman villa sites generally took advantage of the natural landscape for whatever reason – and this site certainly did.

During the two seasons of work, our investigations revealed a typical Romano-British site from the 4th century AD comprising the solid base for a possible grand entrance, perhaps arched and mostly constructed of flint bonded with mortar and clay. There was also a boundary wall of similar but crude construction on the southern upper slopes. These were flanked by a boundary ditch to the east and west within the lower levels, and a well-constructed large barn, perhaps used as a stable, made up of flint and lime mortar, which showed no signs of domestic activity. The pitched roof of this building is likely to have been covered with *tegula* and *imbrex* roof tile. It was located immediately to the east of the main entrance as one entered the projected villa grounds from the south.

The villa within its dramatic landscape. (DS)

An artist's impression of the villa building and complex viewed from the south. (LSH)

Looking across the site, in my mind I could almost appreciate what the villa and its bath house – positioned on the opposite side of the field to the north upslope – must have looked like. In modern British archaeology, this was a *villa rustica*, or 'countryside villa', commonly referred to now simply as a 'Roman villa'. Most were of the *rustica* type. A villa's design differed depending on the architect and the needs of the original client.

Looking across from the southern entrance into the immediate estate grounds, there may well have been a garden fronting the south side of the villa complex. Pleasure gardens typified the art of fine living during Roman times.

Pliny the Elder used the term *opus topiarium*, which was derived from the Greek word *topia* (landscapes). Pliny listed a great variety of gardens as 'groves, woods, hills, fish pools, canals, rivers, coasts'. The Romans also introduced garden furniture, formal layouts, the shaping of trees and the combination of plants with perhaps a water display. Trees and plants were cultivated in ornamental gardens with an emphasis on greenery rather than floral display. A villa in Roman times, as at Mud Hole, was the cultural ideal of rural life – a humble and peaceful yet impressive Romano-British retreat.

Sometimes, on a quiet evening after all the hardworking volunteers had left site, I would reflect on the day's productive fieldwork, and the findings of the day within this peaceful setting. Both seasons of fieldwork were completed on a tight schedule, so there was always much to think about. Yet I could never imagine prior to the dig commencing in 2017 what we were soon to find. This was to become a very real Howard Carter moment for me. I had often joked about it with the volunteers, especially with the late Andrew Lyle. "One day we will find a mosaic" I would say…!

Anyway, our excavations revealed the villa to be of modest size with a floor plan covering a total area of approximately 260 square metres. It had perhaps been a two-storey building rendered on the outside with red brick coursing visible, seen with the discovery of buttressing found butting the north-east corner of the main villa. The lower part of the main villa structure was likely to have shown faced flint pointed with a lime mortar. This was observed to the rear of the building on the north side. The

The Howard Carter moment in 2017 as we get our first glimpse of a mosaic. (NB)

building was probably covered with large grey worked sandstone roof tiles on its pitched roof, and solid roof timbers. Its adjoining later addition of a bath house at its western end may have had a domed roof constructed of locally sourced lightweight limestone called *tufa*, typical for bath houses. In addition, there was a front corridor which was perhaps utilised as a *portico* due to the crude construction of its south-facing foundation wall. The *portico* or corridor probably supported a pitched roof covered with *tegula* and *imbrex* roof tile and was held up either with timber posts or stone columns. At the western end of the *portico*, the corridor contained a small but what must have been an enclosed plunge pool lined with the waterproof cement called *opus signinum*. This may have led any guest into or out of the main bath house area. Near to the main entrance there may well have been a *Lararium*, which contained a shrine dedicated to the *Lares*. These were household gods who protected the family. Food and drink may have been placed in front of their images.

Someone entering the main building through the entrance along Trench 1 could then turn right and go through a 2m-wide doorway, where the remains of a column base was found, into a 6m x 5m room. This space is likely to have functioned as a *Tablinum or Triclinium* which was separated from the main entrance room usually by an array of columns or half columns (pilasters) and had retractable

A detail of the flint external wall. (DS)

A buttress to the north-east of the building. (DS)

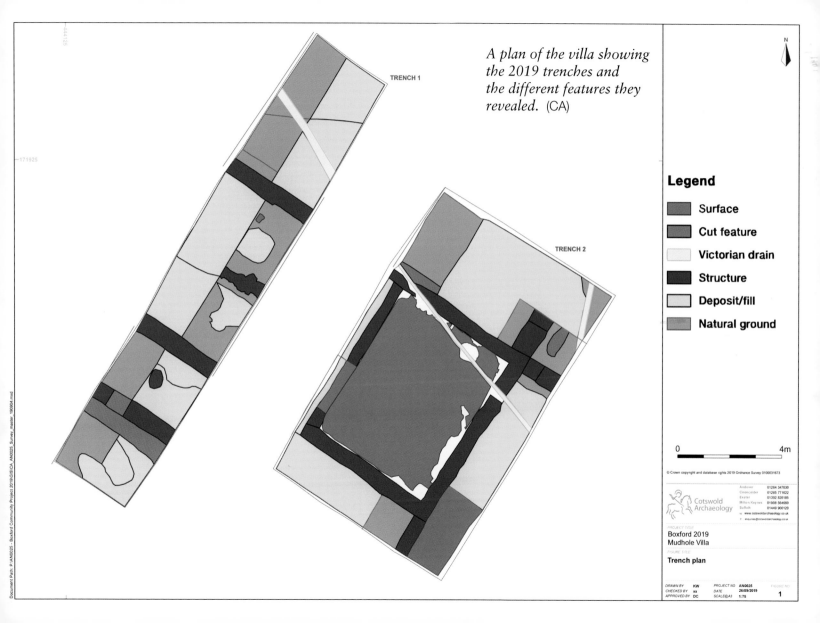

A plan of the villa showing the 2019 trenches and the different features they revealed. (CA)

TRENCH 1

TRENCH 2

Legend

Surface

Cut feature

Victorian drain

Structure

Deposit/fill

Natural ground

0   4m

© Crown copyright and database rights 2019 Ordnance Survey 0100031673

Cotswold Archaeology

Andover	01264 347630
Cirencester	01285 771022
Exeter	01392 826185
Milton Keynes	01908 564660
Suffolk	01449 900120

w www.cotswoldarchaeology.co.uk
e enquiries@cotswoldarchaeology.co.uk

PROJECT TITLE
Boxford 2019
Mudhole Villa

FIGURE TITLE
Trench plan

DRAWN BY	KW	PROJECT NO	AN0025	FIGURE NO.
CHECKED BY	xx	DATE	26/09/2019	
APPROVED BY	DC	SCALE@A3	1:75	**1**

Document Path: P:\AN0025 - Boxford Community Project 2019\GIS\CA_AN0025_Survey_master_190904.mxd doors or portieres (textile hangings). These hangings were draped from the columns to be drawn at will. This cool airy chamber was often used as a dining room but equally may have functioned as a reception room. Green window glass and lead fragments were found in this room suggesting the villa was glazed with lead-lined windows which let a dull green light into its interior during the daytime. There may well have been only a few small windows, as heat was also liable to escape. Box-flue tile fragments were found indicating that the villa may have had heated flooring and/or walls. Glass and heating systems were an expensive commodity and reached the houses of only wealthy aristocrats. Red painted wall plaster fragments were also found within this room space. Interior decoration was an essential ingredient in a Roman lifestyle, transforming and enhancing their living environment. By using the art of perspective in their painting, they enlarged the physical space within a room.

However, the most incredible aspect of this room as one looked down was a superb and well-preserved mosaic floor. This depicted mythological themes and iconography, including Bellerophon killing a fire-breathing monster, and the story of Pelops and his race to win the hand of the Princess Hippodamia. Many of these images had never before been found in Britain. The charm of such a space must have enhanced the private lives of the villa owners and any guest who was visiting. Its magnificent décor advertised the owner's high status. It was also a space in which a variety of activities could take place, from solitary pursuits to great receptions and for storytelling or perhaps discussing business. During the quiet moments, I would try to imagine what life may have been like during Roman times – the building with its mosaic, the man, the family, the people it accommodated, their beliefs, the scenic views they enjoyed across their immediate estate grounds and the gossip of the day.

The successful public open day in September 2019 was

The entrance to the mosaic room – note the stone column base fragment. (DS)

The Victorian land drain which luckily only cut through the fringe of the mosaic. (DS)

the highlight of all this work and certainly brought the site, with the mosaic, back to life to be enjoyed again by the many thousands of people who visited, just as it must have been nearly 1,700 years ago. All of us who took part in the community dig at Boxford are very proud of what we uncovered and achieved.

Rome, the Republic and the rise and fall of an Empire

In order to understand the villa at Mud Hole, and its eventual demise, we need to look at the complexities of Rome and of Roman Britain (*Britannia*) during the 4th century AD, shortly before Roman rule officially ended in Britain in 410 AD.

Rome

The city of Rome, the capital of the Roman Empire, governed a vast area that stretched in the north to present-day Scotland, to Syria and parts of Asia in the east, North Africa to the south and Spain to the west. Rome and its powerful elite ruled from between 60 to 120 million people. The Roman army was the most powerful in the world, and as it conquered more and more land, the empire increased its wealth by exploiting the resources of each new conquered territory. Rome grew into a breathtaking capital of the Roman Empire with ornate marble temples, mesmerising palaces and many forms of entertainment, including spectacular gladiatorial shows, plus sporting and theatrical events to amuse the ever-increasing population. The empire however was never stable during its expansion. There was instability from within, from those that ran its provinces, there were internal civil wars and struggles against the establishment, assassinations, and conflicts of interest between religious beliefs. In addition, external factors such as expensive military campaigns against so-called 'barbarians' all put pressure on Rome's ability to remain peaceful and stable.

Britannia

Roman Britain (*Britannia* in Latin) was governed by the Roman Empire from AD 43 to 410, with London (*Londinium*) becoming its largest planned town. Britain comprised almost the whole of what is now England and Wales and, for a short period, southern Scotland. Rome considered the conquest of Britain necessary. Julius Caesar invaded Britain in 55 and 54 BC as part of his Gallic Wars. According to Caesar, the Britons had been overrun by other Celtic tribes during the Iron Age and these had been aiding his enemies. He received tribute, installed a friendly king, and returned to Gaul. Yet although Caesar had dismissed the island as having little of value, the truth was far from it. Not only was Britain important for tax revenue but it was also valuable for its mineral resources – tin, iron, and gold – as well as hunting dogs and animal furs. As with other regions that had fallen to the empire, grain, cattle, and slaves were also there to be exploited. For example, the Emperor Diocletian's price edict in AD 301 shows that at least two British cloth products had won an empire-wide reputation. For these reasons, in AD 43 the Emperor Claudius directed four legions to invade Britain on the pretext of restoring the exiled king Verica over the Atrebates tribe. Verica was an Iron Age chieftan and ally of the empire. The Romans were successful, so they pushed north and defeated the neighbouring Catuvellauni tribe with further conquests northwards during the first century AD.

Britannia and the Roman Empire in the 3rd Century AD

During the latter half of the 3rd century AD, Rome's Imperial Crisis was characterised by constant civil war, as various military leaders fought for control of the empire. Social unrest and economic pressures divided the empire into separate regions. The Emperor Diocletian came up with the idea of creating four leaders, or Tetrarchs, in multiple locations. Each would have significant power and the death of one of the Tetrarchs would not mean a change in governance. This new approach would reduce the risk of assassination and made it nearly impossible to overthrow the entire empire.

Despite this reorganisation, Diocletian divided the Empire in half in AD 285 and elevated one of his officers, Maximian, to the position of co-emperor. By doing this, Diocletian created the Western Roman Empire and the Eastern Roman Empire. Successors were to be chosen and approved from the outset of an individual's rule – with Diocletian making his pick the generals Maxentius and Constantine.

In AD 305, Diocletian voluntarily retired, and the Tetrarchy was dissolved as rival regions of the Empire fought with each other for dominance. Following Diocletian's death in AD 311, Maxentius and Constantine plunged the empire again into civil war.

Opposite: The mosaic room showing the surrounding flint-based walls dug into the landscape. (DS)

In AD 312, Emperor Constantine defeated Maxentius and the Praetorian faction under the Sign of the Cross at the Battle of the Milvian Bridge and became sole ruler of both the Western and Eastern Empires. This point marks the official conversion of Rome to Christianity, as well as the dissolution of the ancient Praetorian Guards themselves. Constantine believed that Jesus Christ was responsible for his victory and initiated a series of laws, such as the Edict of Milan in AD 317 which commissioned religious tolerance throughout the empire. In the same way that earlier Roman emperors had claimed a special relationship with a deity or god to augment their authority (Caracalla with Serapis or Diocletian with Jupiter), Constantine chose the figure of Jesus Christ. At the First Council of Nicea in AD 325, he codified the Christian faith and ensured manuscripts would be collected that would eventually form The Bible. Constantine stabilised the empire, revalued the currency, reformed the military, as well as founding the city he called New Rome (Constantinople) on the site of the former city of Byzantium (modern-day Istanbul).

Following the death of Constantine, there was a period of civil war throughout the empire but in AD 353, the empire was once again united under a single ruler, Constantius II. Britain was returned to Imperial rule but in AD 360 there were some major upsets in northern Britain from the Picts and Scots, who launched raids across the frontier in defiance of a peace agreement. In addition to this, Rome increasingly had to confront the threat from barbarian tribes in the East, and Britain found itself with undermanned defences, unable to protect itself against determined enemy attacks.

Barbarians

The Romans called all the people who lived outside the Roman Empire 'barbarians'. The very meaning of the word still conjures up someone who may be uncivilised or primitive. Indeed, recent media coverage has used this word to describe various terrorist factions and their atrocities. In Roman times, the so called barbarians along the Rhine frontier in particular had been feared for several hundred years. The

A Roman coin from Emperor Constans (AD347-348) found in Trench 1. (CF)

main reason for this was the massive defeat of the Roman army under Varus in 9 AD. The Battle of the Teutoburg Forest cost Rome three legions and over 15,000 men. Many of the Germanic tribes were subsequently subdued but Rome kept away from pushing further eastwards – allowing the Rhine to become a natural frontier. That Germanic victory, along with the later loss of some 5,000 of the Ninth Legion beyond the northern frontier of Britain, would have far-reaching psychological effects on the subsequent history of the peoples of the Roman Empire.

The Fall of Britannia and the Roman Empire

In the 4th century AD, the Roman Army had considerable difficulty stopping these barbarians from entering the Roman Empire. The Romans were forced to increase the size of their army. By the end of the 4th century AD, the army had grown to 600,000 men, 250,000 of which were stationed on Rome's northern borders. Taxation had to be increased to pay for such a large army, but these taxes were higher than most people could afford and created wide-scale poverty. Some people were forced to sell their children into slavery, while others died of starvation. Plague also became a problem and during one outbreak, people in Rome were dying at the rate of 5,000 a day. The population of the Roman Empire began to fall dramatically and this in turn reduced the numbers of people available to join the army. Despite these problems, agricultural production throughout the empire was the powerhouse of the economy during that time, especially as it was needed to feed the military. Many farmers exploited this need and it provided the foundations of both power and status during the late Roman period.

The Roman military, manned largely with barbarian mercenaries who had no ethnic ties to Rome, could no longer safeguard the borders as efficiently as they once had, nor could the government as easily collect taxes in the provinces. Further, the debasement of the currency, begun under the Severan Dynasty, had steadily encouraged inflation. Slave labour deprived lower-class citizens of jobs so unemployment levels soared too. The arrival of the Visigoths in the empire in the 3rd century AD, fleeing from invading German tribes, has also been cited as a contributing factor in the decline.

From AD 376-382, Rome fought a series of battles against invading Goths known today as the Gothic Wars. At the Battle of Adrianople, AD 378, the Roman Emperor Valens was defeated resulting in the decline of the Western Roman Empire. In AD 383, the usurper Magnus Maximus withdrew troops from northern and western Britain, probably leaving local warlords in charge. The final Roman withdrawal from Britain occurred around AD 410. The Romano-British expelled the magistrates of the usurper Constantine III, ostensibly in response to his removal of the Roman garrison needed to protect Britain. Roman Emperor Honorius replied to a request for assistance with the *Rescript of Honorius*, telling the Roman cities to see to their own defence, a tacit acceptance of temporary British self-government. Honorius was fighting a large-scale war in Italy against the Visigoths under their leader Alaric, with Rome itself under siege. No forces could be spared to protect distant Britain. Roman control of Britannia was entirely lost. Britain was no longer a province of Rome; however, the years that followed could not erase all of the empire's impact on the people and culture of the island. There was occasional contact with Rome. Missionaries helped Christians battle the heretics, and in the 5th century AD, as attacks from Saxons increased and marauders from Ireland and Scotland raided Roman Britain, an appeal went out to the Roman commanding general Aetius for help. He never replied.

Roman Britain was likely to have been driven into its walled towns and its fortresses, and the open country was now available to Saxons who came as settlers. The only direct mention of London is that of the Anglo-Saxon Chronicle under the year AD 457, when the Britons are said to have sought refuge in the city after their defeat by Hengist at Crecganford (possibly Crayford in Kent). Evidence of the 5th century AD life of St. Germanus, who visited Britain twice, in AD 429 and 447, suggests he found municipal governance still in force in the south-eastern part of Britain. The historical record suggests that towns such as London were able to maintain civic status half a century after the collapse of Britain's rule from Rome. By the second half of the 5th century AD, Roman Britain was struggling...

The End of a Villa...

Britain in the 4th century AD was, on the whole, a period of great prosperity in towns and countryside alike. As

Retrieving the metal stash from the wall. (DS)

A stone roof tile with nail hole from the main roof of the villa. (RM)

A Roman brooch (probably copper alloy) found at the villa. (CF)

discussed, the military needed to be fed and many farmers exploited this. The country had escaped the barbarian invasions of the 3rd century so may have seemed a safe refuge for wealthy continentals. But Britain was weak – as control of its defence lay a thousand miles away in Rome, not with local rulers. By the end of the 4th century AD, whatever the state of Britain's towns, the countryside had to a large extent lost the best of its Roman elements as Imperial rule collapsed. No Romano-British country house seems to show evidence of occupation after the third quarter of the 4th century AD, except for those that clung to their old way of life. The collapse appears to

have put an end to Romano-British country life on any significant scale.

At Mud Hole Villa, excavations revealed that before the main roof and corridor roof collapsed, the portico or corridor floor had been robbed of any useful material and the main central room next to the mosaic had changed function. It too had suffered the same fate as the corridor floor, robbed of its floor matrix in favour of a compact chalk floor laid down afterwards so the room could perhaps be used for storage or to hold livestock.

Several crude but solid foundations were found, one in

the front corridor and one in the main central room, which suggests these acted as supports for upright timbers to hold the roof up during the demise of the building.

A rare iron hoard of door hinges and brackets had been placed within the lower course of the mosaic's eastern external wall within what was likely to have functioned as an inbuilt drainage channel. This suggests the doors and other internal elements of the building had been stripped of any valuable material and hidden from view.

For some reason the iron fittings were never retrieved. The mosaic too had also suffered fire damage at some point before the roof tile collapsed, either from squatter occupation or an internal upper floor fire.

Much of the bath house floor levels had succumbed to plough damage and there was tentative evidence to suggest this area had been looted. A large robber pit was discovered within the bath house complex and numerous artefacts were found to suggest activity continued at the site even after the building had finally fallen into disuse, collapsed and been robbed of valuable building material.

Despite all the destruction at this Boxford villa, as with many other villa sites found in Britain, the mosaic had by some miracle survived. Had it been discovered in Victorian times, casual exposure and frost could have put paid to its majesty. Luckily, it is now safely covered over, but with its glory largely intact – and carefully recorded for posterity.

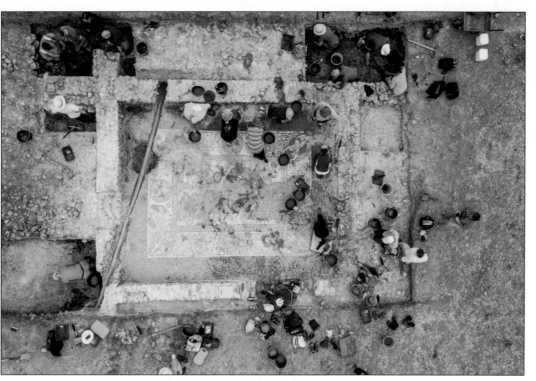

The team at work on the villa. (DS)

THE MYTHS OF THE MOSAIC:
THE TRIUMPHS OF PELOPS AND BELLEROPHON

By Anthony Beeson

The mid-4th century Roman mosaic uncovered at Mud Hole, Boxford in 2017 and 2019 has proven to be the most innovative and delightful ever discovered in Britain. Its subject matter and design is unmatched in the country, and with its riot of twenty-eight figured depictions of characters from Greco-Roman mythology, it appears to all intent and purpose to be a Mediterranean pavement set under English skies.

The two main subjects of the mosaic's central panel feature the stories of Pelops' quest to marry the Princess Hippodamia and the triumph of the hero Bellerophon over the monster Chimaera. The surrounding border is filled by subjects that in most cases seem to be connected to these or to Poseidon (Neptune), the god of the sea and the creator of the horse. Almost every subject is unmatched in Britain thus far.

Like most mosaics the decorative centre is surrounded by a border of coarse terracotta tesserae (stones) whose purpose was to hold the furniture that was anciently placed around the edges of a room so as not to damage the mosaic. A rectangular band of guilloche (ropework) pattern surrounds the important central panels but, unlike on most mosaics, this is dispensed with or overstepped when subjects or inscriptions take priority. The mosaicists worked by eye and not rulers so inscriptions (in themselves rare) are untidily fitted in.

The Central Panel

Bellerophon

The centre of the mosaic is occupied by story panels aligned in different directions. Facing the presumed south entrance, and presumably the first to confront the visitor, is a panel showing the hero Bellerophon, mounted on the flying horse Pegasus, in the act of slaying the monstrous, fire-breathing Chimaera. The latter had the head and body of a lion but from its back grew the head of a goat and its tail was a venomous serpent. It is the finest rendition of the story to have been found in Britain and the most painterly and vibrant.

The Myth

The story of Bellerophon, like that of Pelops, is one of the oldest in western civilisation. Bellerophon, Prince of Corinth,

Diagrams of the characters within the full mosaic

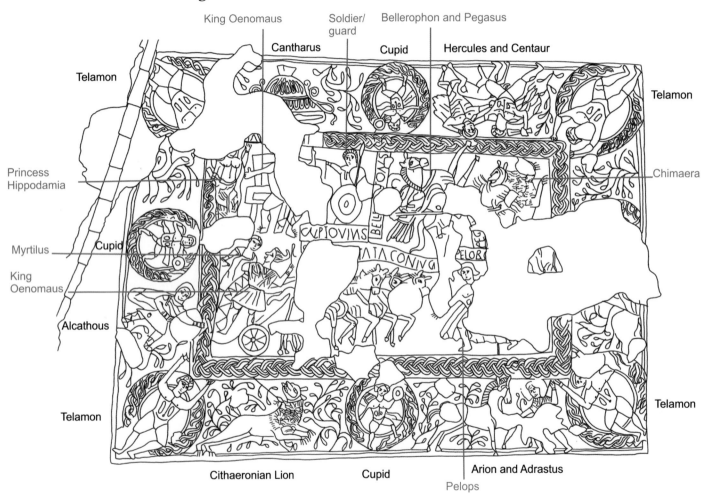

King Oenomaus

Soldier/ guard

Bellerophon and Pegasus

Cantharus

Cupid

Hercules and Centaur

Telamon

Telamon

Princess Hippodamia

Chimaera

Myrtilus

Cupid

King Oenomaus

Alcathous

Telamon

Telamon

Cithaeronian Lion

Cupid

Arion and Adrastus

Pelops

was the natural son of the Greek sea god Poseidon (Neptune in Roman mythology) by his mortal mother, Eurynome, although he passed for the child of King Glaucus of Corinth. Having been accused of murder, he was sent to the court of King Proetus of Tiryns who, by virtue of his kingship, cleansed his young guest of the crime. Unfortunately, Bellerophon's beauty and valour inflamed Proetus' wife, Anteia (also known as Stheneboea) who made advances to him. Infuriated by Bellerophon's rejection, Anteia told Proetus that his guest had attempted to seduce her. But the deeply ingrained Greek concept of hospitality, known as *xenia* or 'guest-friendship', made it impossible for Proetus to kill his guest. So he sent Bellerophon to Anteia's father, King Iobates of Lycia, with a sealed letter requesting that he be put to death. However Iobates left it too long to open the message and so again was forbidden by custom to kill a guest. He therefore sent Bellerophon on a quest to kill the terrifying Chimaera who was ravaging the flocks of Lycia in the hope that he would not return.

Chimaera was the progeny of the primordial monsters Typhon and Echidna. Her body was that of a maned lion but, from her back, sprang the head of a goat. A living serpent formed her tail. All three heads – lion, goat and snake – breathed fire. Aided by Athena (Minerva) and with her gift of a golden, calming bridle, Bellerophon had mastered the flying horse Pegasus (who was in fact his half-brother) when he came to drink at the Peirene spring in Corinth. It is of course unusual to have an equine half-brother but his father Poseidon had seduced the once-beautiful Medusa in the temple of virgin goddess Athena. Scandalised by the affront, the goddess turned the girl's hair into writhing serpents and thereafter all who met Medusa's gorgon stare were turned to stone. When Perseus (on his own quest) cut off Medusa's head, her offspring with Poseidon – the fully formed half-brothers to Bellerophon, Pegasus and the humanoid Chrysaor – sprang out of her decapitated neck. Pegasus was born at the *pegae* or 'springs of the ocean' near Libya which gave him his name. He was also blessed with the power to strike the ground with his hooves and bring forth inspiring springs. Chrysaor married Callirrhoe, the daughter of the Titan god Oceanus. Their son was the triple-bodied warrior Geryon whom Hercules slew with a poisoned arrow while stealing his cattle on the tenth labour.

Mounted on Pegasus, Bellerophon sought out Chimaera and they finally dispatched her by thrusting a lance tipped with lead into one of her fiery throats. The lead melted and, searing her vitals, killed her. After several more adventures together on quests set by Iobates, Bellerophon was finally seen to be virtuous and was awarded the hand of the king's daughter, Philonoe. Alas, pride in his semi-divine origins and victories were to be Bellerophon's downfall. He attempted to fly on Pegasus to join the gods on Olympus, but Pegasus, unsettled at the impiety or stung by a gadfly sent by Zeus (Jupiter), threw him and he fell back to earth. Thereafter lame and embittered, he served as an example of hubris to mankind. Pegasus was himself welcomed by the Gods and he thereafter transported the thunderbolts used by Zeus. Eventually his image was set amongst the stars as a constellation.

Left: An aerial view of the Bellerophon panel. (DS)
Right: An interpretive reconstruction of the missing areas of the panel. Note the lead-covered lance that Bellerophon plunges into fire from the monster's goat head which proves fatal for Chimaera. (AB)

35

The Mosaic

The story of Bellerophon, told in Homer's Iliad (book vi. 155-202), was particularly popular in Britannia and this is the fifth depiction to have been discovered here. Others are known from Lullingstone (Kent), Hinton St Mary and Frampton (Dorset) and Croughton (Northamptonshire). Considering that under thirty mosaics of the subject have been found throughout the Empire, the fact that five have been found here is interesting. The iconography of Bellerophon defeating Chimaera gradually developed into that of St George and the Dragon, so it seems particularly pertinent that the myth was popular in Britain. An ancient belief saw Pegasus as the sun and Chimaera as winter. Bellerophon, as the active power of the sun, attacks winter and thus arranges the sequence of the seasons. In late antiquity, a landowner might wish to be flatteringly identified with the hero before his tenants and clients. The image also came to be seen as the power of good conquering evil and as such it was adopted into early Christian art.

Bellerophon and Chimaera appear on Archaic Greek pottery from the 7th century BC and on early pebble mosaics from the 4th century BC. The basic composition hardly changed over the centuries. However by the late 4th century AD, unlike the traditional mosaic depictions where Bellerophon is heroically naked apart from a hat, boots and a cloak, the hero began to be portrayed in contemporary dress. Boxford's hero is fully clothed in a fashionable 4th century white tunic, complete with blue wristbands, decorative *orbiculi* (roundels) and *clavi* (stripes). The latter decorate the tunic's neckline and the orbiculi appear at the shoulder as well as the thigh. Such decoration is commonplace on contemporary figures on the mosaics at Piazza Armerina in Sicily.

Unfortunately Bellerophon's head has been destroyed beyond one blue tessera indicating the position of his chin, but most of the composition remains, although in places discoloured by burning. Only the mosaic from Croughton (tentatively dated to around 360AD) features a clothed Bellerophon in Britain. Boxford's Bellerophon holds a spear in his right hand that ends above the goat's head. A row of white tesserae define his left shoulder for the viewer and the heel of Bellerophon's boot survives below Pegasus' belly. He wears a red *chlamys* (cloak) across one shoulder that billows out in front of him displaying its lining. This feature consists of swirls of red and pink-brown with a curved line of blue near the centre indicating that billowing fabric is intended here and certainly not a shield as some have suggested which would be iconographically incorrect. Elsewhere on the central panels, fabrics are given a similar multi-colour treatment to indicate linings and at Hinton St Mary, Dorset, Bellerophon's cloak also billows before him. Here it billows to the right so as not to clutter the area behind him occupied by Pegasus' wings.

Inscriptions on mosaic are rare in Britain but above this

Opposite: Details of Bellerophon's garments and Pegasus' harness. The mosaicist uses white tesserae to add depth to his figures. Here a shoulder is outlined behind Pegasus' head to distinguish it from the billowing cloak. (AB)

panel are the letters 'BELLE[RE]FONS'. Only portions of the bracketed letters remain but enough to be certain that this is correct. The same spelling of the name occurs on a 4th century AD Bellerophon mosaic from the Villa de Puerta Oscura, Malaga in Spain.

Dr Roger Tomlin, of the Centre for the Study of Ancient Documents, who kindly studied the inscriptions comments on the Bellerophon inscription

"The inscription: 'BELLE[RE]FONS' like the picture it captions is intended to be read by someone entering the room from the south. This describes the scene below, of Bellerophon killing Chimaera. The F has a wide lower serif, as if it were E. This may be another of the mosaicist's muddles, but F is quite often written with a long leftward serif which may extend to the right; and the upper horizontal stroke of F is extended right, further than those below it. To the left of F, enough survives of the white ground to exclude the expected O. Instead, as Anthony points out, there are two black tesserae in just the right position for the top horizontal stroke of E. 'Bellerophon' thus is spelled 'BELLEREFONS' as in the Malaga mosaic (Pallarès 1997 = Hispania Epigraphica website, Inscr. No. 2882)."

Pegasus

Boxford's figure of Pegasus is without doubt the most spirited and beautiful yet discovered in Britain. His most notable feature is a marvellous mane composed of a series of strikingly long, and often tapering, blue and ochre tesserae laid in alternating colours. This beautiful way of treating horses' manes occurs elsewhere on this mosaic and is one of the most singular techniques attributed to this mosaicist. The same technique is used for Pegasus' long and sinuous tail composed of nine alternate blue and ochre strands. The wings, which often caused mosaicists difficulty in fitting around a rider, are treated as two sets of flipper-like objects that splay out behind Bellerophon. At the top of each wing is a long protruding flight feather and they are striped with blue, brown and white tesserae. Neither of the Pegasus figures on Bellerophon mosaics discovered at Frampton and Hinton St Mary in Dorset featured wings, so Boxford joins Lullingstone and Croughton's mosaicists in attempting them. Lullingstone's are the most elegant but its

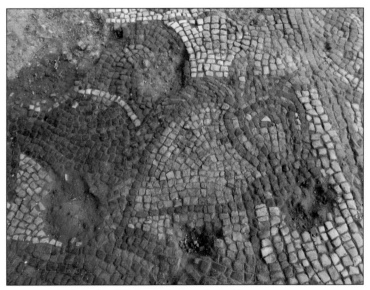

A detail of Pegasus's head and harness. (AB)

Pegasus is the most vapid. Our Pegasus' body is worked in ochre tesserae with muscles and wings outlined in blue. His muzzle is ochre with blue detailing and once would have had a red nostril like the other horses on the pavement. Apart from the singular treatment of horses' manes, the Boxford mosaicist generally employs triangular tesserae to form the whites of his figures' eyes and Pegasus is no exception.

Traditionally, Athena presented Bellerophon with a golden bridle to capture Pegasus and the use of red on the horse may allude to this. Red reins lead from blue bit rings. He sports a red bridle and breast band whilst a red haunch strap disappears beneath Bellerophon from a haunch junction at his hindquarters. A red pendant strap with a circular ornament hangs from the junction and a breeching strap continues under the tail. What is unique is the mosaicist's attempt to give another dimension to the steed as he is shown literally in a flying gallop leaping out of the panel with his left front leg reaching to the outer edge of the guilloche border. The triangular undersides of the hooves are displayed to aid the illusion. Similarly his hind legs stretch out behind, crossing into the neighbouring panel with the fetlocks terminating its long inscription box. Unlike on the cruder Bellerophon mosaic from Croughton, there are no possible references to Pegasus' later catasterism (placement in the heavens as a constellation) or to the horse's spring-striking propensities. The depiction par excellence for the horse's latter ability must surely be the Bellerophon mosaic found at Palmyra in 2005, where water pours from his hooves as a weapon to extinguish Chimaera's fiery breath.

What remains of another name box below the figure of Bellerophon's steed retains all or part of the letters 'PEGAS[vs]'. In the area of the hindquarter's pendant, the mosaic has received a tremendous blow from either a beam or curved stone object falling from a great height, which gives one some idea of the proportions of the chamber. The blow has not destroyed the tessellation but has compressed a semicircle of it allowing one to study the immediate underlying foundation layer. Surprisingly, the mortared mosaic floor was laid down on a 25-30mm layer of reddish sand. The heavy blow on Pegasus' image (delightfully shaped like the striking of a horse's hoof) has compressed the mosaic into this sand.

Chimaera

Below Pegasus is the figure of Chimaera, mostly drawn in blue outline. Damage and burning have obfuscated some details but most of it survives up to the animal's lower back. The back claws and part of its outstretched legs survive on a mosaic island stretching into the open zone of the adjacent panel. When first discovered in 2017, and before cleaning, the portion of the Boxford Chimaera then viewed did not seem to be laid to the same standard as those of Bellerophon and Pegasus above it and the author doubted that it was the work of the same mosaicist in the firm. With cleaning and full excavation that first opinion has changed. Naïve it certainly is but it is full of vigour and, when intact, must have possessed the same charm as that of the western border's Cithaeronian Lion on which she is obviously based, and that delighted all who viewed it upon discovery.

Chimaera is depicted as running at high speed with outstretched limbs and drooping claws, but also turning and defiantly attacking her tormentors. All of the British examples, with the exception of Croughton's, show a fleeing Chimaera. Lullingstone's rather resembles an otter in size and ferocity while (judging by Hinton St Mary's) the Dorset examples resemble sedated string puppets. From the Boxford Chimaera's mouths, decreasingly curved rays of fire shoot forth that in design rather remind one of a heat ray in a comic book

The Etruscan bronze figure of Chimaera from Arezzo now in the National Archaeological Museum of Florence dates from around 400 BC. (AB)

or a child's drawing of a fir tree. The forelimbs stretch out towards the panel's corner and below the creature's wavy lion mane. Although Chimaera was female she had a mane but not one that obscured the ears. The lion head suggests that the mosaicist had no personal knowledge of that species. Its open jaws are full of fire and, unlike the Cithaeronian Lion, no teeth are depicted. The goat's head has suffered damage at its neck and discolouration but details can be made out. It looks backwards at the attacker and has two rectangular ears, and below its chin, a double beard. What originally was interpreted as a triangular wattle now appears as part of its throat. Only a fragment of the white of its eye remains. Of the serpent tail, only a section of the throat and lower jaw together with some flames survives to the upper left of the goat's head. On the remaining part of her belly, two of a series of spaced teats survive, formed from single blue tesserae. With the evidence provided from the fragment of hind limbs and claws that survives, the remaining part of the creature can be successfully restored by referring to the depiction of the lion in the western border.

Chimaera's inscription has been lost but was probably situated above the fire-burst from the lion's head and below Pegasus' front right leg where the corner of a

Opposite: The three heads of Chimaera. Only a fragment of the throat and lower jaw of the serpent head survives to the left above the central goat's head. (AB)

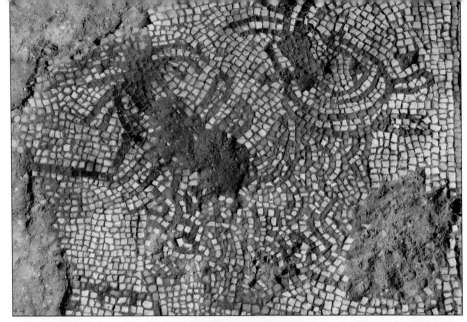

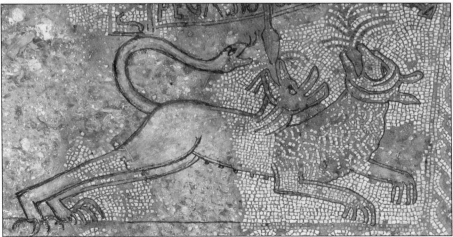

rectangular frame remains. The author's photographs and onsite tracings show that this frame is on a different alignment to that of the Pegasus inscription to which it abuts. It is also not of the same height. With reference to the mosaic from Malaga, that likewise uses the same, and unique, spelling of 'BELLEREFONS' as at Boxford, Chimaera there is written as 'QVMERA' which fits perfectly into this small frame and may also be how it appeared here.

Discussing this with Roger Tomlin and how to restore it in the reconstruction drawing he wrote:

"I quite see why you read QVMERA: it is certainly there in the photo you sent me, and I was following a less accurate drawing. What puzzles me is that the standard publication in *The Corpus Inscriptionum Latinarum*, CIL II (6338p) reads CIMERA, and so does J G Pallares, *Edicion y comentario de las inscripciones sobre mosaic de Hispania* (1997).

CIMERA is much more plausible as a western-provincial rendering of Greek Chimaera than the Q-version, although I don't know about Spanish peculiarities. QV sometimes becomes C, as in comodo for quomodo, but I can't believe in CHI becoming

QV. In Roman Britain, at least, CIMERA is altogether plausible."

So we were no further forward until he wrote to me again:

"I have now consulted Pallarès and J. Blazquez, *Mosaicos Romanos de Cordoba, Jaen y Malaga* (1981), and I find you are quite right: the mosaic does indeed read QV|ME|RA, which Pallarès expands as QV(i)|ME|RA. Blazquez has the better photograph, and the first letter there is undoubtedly

Bellerophon captures Pegasus with the aid of Athena.
(Painting from Pompeii; Regio. 1.8.9.)

The fall of Bellerophon by Dimitrios Biskinnis on a Greek Postage stamp. (AB)

Q. The odd thing is, in both their commentaries they do not comment on the spelling but simply refer to 'la Quimera', which I now find is the modern spelling of the word in Spanish.

I take it that the form C(h)im(a)era (i.e. CIMERA) in secondary accounts such as CIL II is a learned 'correction'. But I still commend CIMERA to you. It would be slightly narrower than QVMERA, and could be narrowed a little more if necessary, by ligaturing E to R or (less likely) by inserting a small I within C. If E were ligatured to R, its three horizontals would be attached to the upright of R. Alternatively, they might have been attached to M. In either case, the upright of E would be suppressed. But I think a ligature unlikely, unless he was really pressed for space. But CIMERA (to repeat myself) is entirely acceptable as a Romano-British 'Vulgarism', whereas QVMERA is not. It must be an 'Iberian' form, although even Blazquez refers obscurely to another mosaic which has Bellerophon killing the 'CIMERA'..... So, unless you would like to find an itinerant Spanish mosaic-artist in Britain, I suggest you restore CIMERA to the frame."

This interesting discussion with Roger brings to the fore the question of why the hero's name was spelled at Boxford in a manner that is only found on this one Spanish mosaic. Was the cartoon that the possibly illiterate mosaicist worked from or the codex that it might have been based on of Spanish origin, or can we really believe that either he or the patron was of Iberian origins?

The Triumph of Pelops
The Myth

The characters in the story of Pelops are again some of the earliest in Greek mythology and predate those in the Bellerophon tale. Poseidon and horses again feature. Pelops was the son of King Tantalus of Sipylus in Lydia, although some say his real father was in fact the titan Atlas. Originally Tantalus was a friend of Zeus and sat at his table, but he shared his secrets and the divine food of Ambrosia and Nectar with his mortal friends and would fall from favour. Worse occurred when he invited the gods to a banquet and murdered and cut up his son Pelops to bulk out a stew to be served to them. All recoiled in horror but Demeter (Ceres), who was distracted and mourning for her abducted daughter, Persephone, ate part of his shoulder. For his crimes, Tantalus was sentenced to the everlasting torment of hunger and thirst within reach of food and water.

Zeus had Hermes (Mercury) gather up Pelops' remains and they were again boiled in the same cauldron under a spell and reassembled. Demeter replaced the shoulder she had eaten with a magic ivory one. The youth that emerged from the cauldron was so beautiful that Poseidon fell in love with him and took him to Olympus at once to be his cup bearer and lover. Later when Zeus discovered the truth about Tantalus' theft of divine food, Pelops was banished from Olympus and returned to his kingdom. He was driven from it by Tros the king of Troy, who was searching for his beautiful son Ganymede whom Zeus in eagle form had abducted to be his cup bearer and bedfellow. Tros believed that the House of Tantalus had abducted him.

Pelops therefore travelled to Greece where he had heard that Hippodamia, the beautiful daughter of King Oenomaus of Pisa and Elis, was available for marriage. Ancient Pisa equates with the modern village of Miraka and lay a kilometre from the sanctuary at Olympia. Oenomaus (whose name translates as 'man of wine') was a great lover of horses. His daughter's name means 'Horse Tamer' and he forbad any of his subjects to pollute horses by mating their mares with asses to produce mules. Some say Oenomaus was the son of Ares (Mars) by Sterope, again a child of the heaven-supporting titan Atlas, and others say that he married her. Either of these theories may account for the presence of the *atlantes* or *telamones* – male figures who appear to hold up the four corners of the mosaic above their heads. Unfortunately for those who wished to marry Hippodamia, her father had been told by an oracle that a future son-in-law would bring about his death and so he was determined that none would wed her. Others said that the king himself was enamoured of his own daughter and did not want her to marry.

As a skilled charioteer, he challenged all suitors to a chariot race but stipulated that any who lost would be put to death. He also insisted that Hippodamia should ride in their chariots, which naturally distracted and handicapped them. The designated course ran from Pisa down to Poseidon's altar on the Isthmus. Although competitors were given a good start whilst the king sacrificed to Zeus at Olympia, his chariot was designed for racing and his team included the divine horses Psylla and Harpinna who were swifter than Boreas the North Wind and given to him by his father Ares. Oenomaus always caught the competitors and speared them before they finished the course. Up to eighteen suitors perished and their heads were nailed to the wooden pillars of the palace.

When Pelops heard of the race he begged his former lover Poseidon's aid 'for the sake of Aphrodite's sweet gifts', and the god lovingly sent him a golden chariot pulled by winged horses that could fly across the sea. Notwithstanding this gift, Pelops was unnerved by the sight of the severed heads when he reached the palace, although from the first glance both he and the princess desired one another. He therefore bribed Myrtilus, a son of Hermes (Mercury) and Oenomaus' chariot master, to aid him with promises of half his kingdom and the first night with Hippodamia following the marriage. Some say that Hippodamia herself also inveigled Myrtilus to aid them. As Myrtilus was himself in love with Hippodamia he agreed and before the race removed one or both metal linchpins from the king's chariot, replacing them with wax copies. At the height of the chase, the wheels flew off Oenomaus' chariot and he was dragged to his death, cursing Myrtilus and wishing the latter to die at the hands of Pelops. Another version has Oenomaus killed by the victorious Pelops at the winning post. Pelops gained the throne and eventually all that part of Greece that would forever enshrine his name as the Peloponnese. The funerary games that he held for Oenomaus and their chariot races became the mythical origins of the Olympic games that were always organised by the people of Elis.

Alas, poor Myrtilus was not to receive his promised reward. Various versions of the tale either see him thrown from the golden chariot into the sea by Pelops after Hippodamia claimed he tried to assault her or thrown from a cliff when the new king went back on his word. As he died he cursed the house of Pelops and its descendants, an invocation for harm that became known as the Curse of the Pelopidai or the Curse of the House of Atreus, which brought repeated tragedy. Hermes, his father, had Myrtilus set amongst the stars as Auriga the charioteer.

The preparations for the chariot race between Oenomaus and Pelops formed the subject for the decoration of the east pediment of the temple of Zeus at Olympia. This is the only large-scale depiction of the story known from antiquity and largely survives in Olympia's museum. The temple itself was the repository for Pheidias' chryselephantine (gold and ivory) statue of Zeus that was one of the Seven Wonders of the World.

The Mosaic – The Court

Only a strip of the Pelops story was uncovered in the excavation of 2017 and the author then believed that what he termed 'The Court Panel' was related to the Triumph of Bellerophon and possibly showed the court of Iobates with the king presenting the Princess Philonoe. It was assumed that perhaps the whole mosaic would be devoted to the Bellerophon story. The 2019 excavation showed that this was not the case. This main section of the mosaic is to be viewed from the western side of the room. A doorway is suspected in the south-western corner but any guest entering from the south, past Bellerophon, would have been led that way to face the Pelops mosaic.

The Court Panel shows Oenomaus seated on his panelled throne which is one of the very few pieces of Roman furniture to be depicted in surviving Romano-British art. Directly above his head, in the outer border, is a *cantharus* (wine cup) as a subtle visual aid to his identification and a play on his name 'Man of Wine'. There was once an inscription above the Court Panel set into the guilloche border of which only a few fragments now survive towards the middle and at the end. As it begins over the figure of the princess I thought that it might name her. Dr Roger Tomlin kindly studied the photographs and tracings made by the author of the remaining letters and passed on his thoughts that are given below.

"On '[...].AV[...]NI' the V is incomplete, but its first stroke is parallel with the second stroke of A, so that V is a reasonable reading. To its left is a letter probably incomplete; only a vertical stroke (H, I, M, N, T). There is not enough room to the left for [HIPPODAM]IA, and the following V makes it still more difficult. So I think

Opposite: The Court of King Oenomaus, with his daughter, Hippodamia, on the left and a guard on the right. Above the scene, in the mosaic's outer border is a 'cantharus' or wine cup that refers to the King's name 'man of wine'. Left (CF). Right (AB).

this must be [OENO]MAV[S]. I can't make anything of what follows, 3 letters lost, and NI. I have suggested REGNI ('of the kingdom'), but only to show how the space might be filled. I can't think of anything more directly relevant to Oenomaus: not the name of his kingdom, and his patronymic would be surely excessive; it doesn't end in NI (genitive) anyway."

Thus [OENO]MAV[S] REGNI is his most likely conclusion for the inscription.

Oenomaus sits in a god-like pose to command awe from the viewer. He is larger than his companions reflecting his importance. Unfortunately, much of his upper body and face are destroyed but enough evidence remains on the mosaic to provide a sensible reconstruction. The line of his neck suggests that his head probably intruded into the inscription above. In his left hand he holds a sceptre or staff of office. A red and buff robe is draped around his body and cascades in folds down between his muscular legs. His feet sport remarkably long and spread toes. A muscle is traced on his upper right arm which he holds out with open palm and upright thumb in a gesture of presentation to direct the viewer to the female figure on the left. This is the Princess Hippodamia.

She is shown in the surprising state of dishabille that virgin princesses adopt in mythological representations but which would have been profoundly shocking in real life. A similarly undressed heroine appears on the mosaic at Nimes, in France, of the bethrothal of Princess Alcestis to Admetus, where the king presents his daughter with just such a gesture as at Boxford and the princess is in exactly the same state of undress. Hippodamia is naked to the groin with her red and buff garment covered in complicated blue folds. She has red armlets and bracelets and holds a billowing scarf. The Boxford mosaicist's ubiquitous pink nipples and navel are evident. Alas she has lost her feet and most of her face above the chin. She intrudes into the guilloche border which ends below her right hand.

To the right of Oenomaus is a figure holding a spear and shield. His hair is fashionably represented by striped tessellation and he wears a contemporary white tunic decorated with bands at the wrist and with clavi at the neck. A red chlamys is draped across one shoulder and his spear intrudes far into the border above. A bossed, oval shield in red and buff rests before him. It is notable that the mosaicist has not bothered to delineate the figure beyond his chest which suggests that he is a subsidiary character in the story. This delightful figure has an importance in that it is the only representation of an armed man with a shield in contemporary mid-4th century dress to be found in Britain. The composition of ruler and armed companion is surely drawn from the sort of imperial imagery seen on the great silver dish made to celebrate the Decennalia in 388 AD, where the emperor and his sons sit enthroned surrounded by the palace guard. The latter stand bare-headed in tunics and bear shields and spears, as is the case with the Boxford figure. He points and looks towards either Hippodamia or to Oenomaus as if directing the viewer's gaze to his majesty. Rather than representing

Pelops or an earlier suitor, this author sees him as a recognisable contemporary scene setter for the solemnity of a ruler's court.

The Mosaic – The Chariot Race

Below Oenomaus, The Court Panel flows into the western half of the mosaic that is concerned with the fatal chariot race. Remarkably only two other mosaic versions of this episode are known in the entire Roman Empire. One from Shaba in Syria featuring the race in the background is now in the National Museum in Damascus and the other has been discovered at a late-antique palace at Noheda (Villar de Domingo García) near Cuenca, Spain. This spectacular late-4th century mosaic again features episodes from the story and may possibly be based on the same original as Boxford's even if considerably removed from it in technique and sophistication. The long rectangular panel at Noheda again features a court scene with Oenomaus, Hippodamia and other members of the story at the left end. Above them hang garlands and the heads of three dead suitors. To the right of this scene, the action bleeds into the story of the race that takes place here in a circus complete with an ornamental central *spina*. The crash is placed next to the Noheda court panel and then, on the far right, is the triumphant Pelops.

At Boxford, the remains of a bearded head hanging from a panel with ansate ends (the sharp corner of one survives) may be seen beneath Hippodamia's feet. The beard echoes the mosaicists' depiction of hair and is composed of overlapping arcs of blue tesserae. Below this is the figure of Myrtilus wearing a high-waisted red and blue striped tunic. In his right hand he holds behind him what was the clue to my interpretation of the mosaic. This pale buff P-shaped object represents the wax linchpin that he would exchange for the metal one. An underlying darker line may represent the latter. His other arm is also depicted behind his body suggesting that he is passing the linchpins between hands. The figure looks (perhaps somewhat shiftily) towards the powerful figure of a charioteer whose face is crudely drawn in profile and depicted as though haranguing Myrtilus. The domineering charioteer's left elbow protrudes stump-like from the sleeve of a short red, white and blue striped tunic. He wields a whip, the end of which appears like the letter N by his hand. Below this, a line represents the draught-pole of the vehicle. He stands in a low-sided Roman racing chariot decorated with a red and blue zig-zag decoration. The horses' red reins are attached to his belt and spread out over the front of the vehicle. The tail of the first horse, formed of long thin tesserae, is outlined in white and flows across the chariot. The vehicle is a *quadriga* or four-horse chariot and the colours of the equine line-up are pink, white and buff. They ready themselves with their left legs raised rather like a chorus line. They mirror Pegasus in execution with their splendid manes and red nostrils but with the addition of red chariot harnesses, breast bands and wide girth straps. Between the legs

An interpretive reconstruction of the chariot panel. Left (CF), Right (AB)

of the pink horse is another impact depression caused by the fall of something from a great height. Again the tesserae survive in the hollow. Matt Nichol, who excavated the hollow, described it as "looking as though one of the telamones had punched it" and indeed it fitted a fist's shape extremely well.

The Boxford charioteer is most likely to be Oenomaus although the mosaicist has misunderstood the iconography and given him a Phrygian cap and a whip, both attributes in art of the Lydian Pelops. Instead of Phrygian trousers he wears a short tunic which would be iconographically incorrect for Pelops. As if to reinforce this, Pelops himself appears at the end of the scene standing at the finishing line. He wears a charioteer's helmet but is heroically nude apart from an open and elaborately decorated robe. He strides forward across the line with his right hand thrust out and the palm spread as if to say 'I am the victor!' Above his head is his name panel misspelled as 'PELOBS'. The uncovering of this confirmed the identification previously made from the linchpin.

Left: King Oenomaus' racing chariot is an authentic low and lightweight Roman version that is buff coloured within and blue outside. It is decorated with a zig-zag pattern. Here, the King appears ebullient and confident of winning the imminent race with Pelops, not knowing that it will be his last. (AB)

An enlargement of the linchpin held by Myrtilus as he stands alongside the king's chariot. (AB)

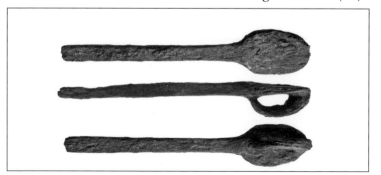

A linchpin. (courtesy Surrey County Council)

On the Noheda mosaic, Myrtilus stands in the same place by a vehicle as at Boxford, but there it is a crashed chariot with fallen horses and a dead king. Above his head in a similar position to the head at Boxford is a detached chariot wheel. If the Boxford head is supposed to be a broken wheel then it bears no comparison in execution with that shown on the chariot. At the end of the Noheda course is the triumphant Pelops in a Phrygian cap and costume standing by Hippodamia in a chariot shown with the same awkward perspective as at Boxford. It seems highly likely that some lost painting of the story, albeit copied into different manuscripts, was the inspiration for both mosaics although the Boxford mosaicist misinterpreted elements of the iconography. Sarcophagi from Cumae (Italy) and Tipasa (Algeria) featuring the Pelops story repeat the Boxford and Noheda formula of depicting a court scene followed by a chariot race which must have been the standard practice in art by the 4th century AD. On the Cumae sarcophagus the victorious

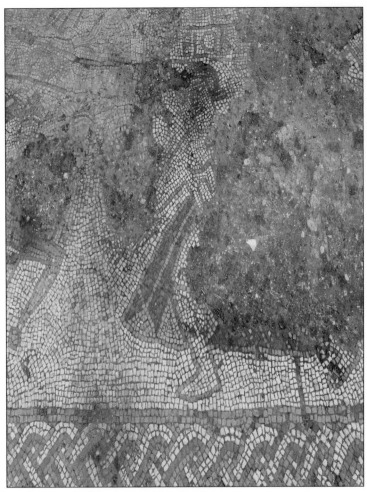

Pelops standing across the finishing line, shown here as a vertical line coming up from below. (AB)

A reconstruction of the Pelops figure. (AB)

A detail of Pelops wearing a charioteer's helmet. (AB)

Pelops himself waves aloft the metal linchpin.

The Mosaic – The Inscription

It is unusual to find inscriptions on British mosaics and Boxford's mosaic has more than most. The major one runs through the Pelops story. Roger Tomlin's interpretation follows.

"(Line 1) CAVLPIO VIVAS or CALIPIO VIVAS

The letters after C are ligatured together, and can be read in various ways:

A extended into L, cut by I, i.e. ALI

AVL, the most straightforward; but odd that the descender of L extends back to A.

The second word is VIVAS, with VA ligatured. 'May you live (many years)'. This might be taken as dependent on CVPIO ('I wish'), but the first-person is intrusive. A sarcastic remark by Oenomaus to a suitor about to die? But I think CVPIO is excluded by the diagonal to the left of V, which must be for A.

VIVAS (and similar) is frequent on silverware (etc.), as an acclamation of good health to the recipient. I think this is its function here.

(Line 2) 'C[...].ATACONIVGE'

Only the upper curve of the first letter. It might be S, but it is just like C above, and I am happy to read C. I am also happy with CONIVGE, ablative of coniunx. The G is just like a reversed D, and I take this to be a mistake by the mosaicist, misinterpreting the sketch in front of him. It shows that he was capable of making visual errors, perhaps because he was illiterate.

The ablative CONIVGE suggests strongly that C is for 'C[VM]', and that the acclamation VIVAS is addressed to someone 'with (your) wife'. The letters before CONIVGE must then be her name. (They end in –A, so this is a feminine name; it is a 'wife', not a 'husband'.) There is a hint of the cross-bar of T in the letter before A, and –ATA is a more likely name-ending than –AIA. Working left, there is the vertical stroke of a letter probably incomplete. I suggest it is N, since –NATA is an easy feminine name-ending. The only other hint as to the name is below the V of VIVAS, and it looks like the top left corner of B, P or R. In my reconstruction, I have suggested that it is R, and have written in FORTVNATA. The spacing suits if one ligatures VN, but of course this is only a plausible guess. But it takes me back to line 1.

CAVLPIO / CALIPIO is the name of the man addressed 'with (your) wife' by the acclamation VIVAS. Neither reading is a plausible name, let alone one which is attested, and I suggest that the mosaicist misinterpreted CAEPIO. He missed the two short upper strokes of E, and thought that the bottom stroke extended from the second stroke of A, producing his unconvincing ligature of A and L interrupted by a vertical. CAEPIO is a perfectly good Latin cognomen, and I suggest the central caption is:

'Caepio vivas
c[um Fo]r[tu]nata coniuge'
'Long life to you, Caepio, with your wife Fortunata'.

Thus Caepio is the name of the villa-owner, and the mosaic is a wedding-present like the obligatory piece of silver, but rather grander. Possibly from his parents-in-law?

Finally, above the figure at the end of the race track.
'PELOBS'
Only the upper curve of P, and the lower curve of S. But B is certain, instead of P. Perhaps another mistake by the mosaicist, unless it goes back to the designer and his cartoon."

Right: The inscriptions 'Long life to you Caepio and to your wife Fortunata' and 'Bellerefons' running at a different angle. (AB)

The Outer Border

The Telamones

The Boxford mosaicist attempted to give his pavement a *trompe l'oeil* or three-dimensional effect. At each corner stands a telamon or giant which, like the female caryatid, was employed on architectural facades instead of columns. The Boxford telamones hold up a rectangular pergola decorated with a guilloche or rope pattern. Telamones, or atlantes, were based on the figure of the mythological giant Atlas, who held up the sky. They seem to have originated in Sicily and colossal examples were used on the façade of the Temple of Zeus at Agrigento. Boxford's telamones are foreshortened to give the appearance of standing upright and they step out of blue cameo guilloche-bordered oval frames or mandorlas that are similarly treated. The guilloche breaks at the top and bottom of the mandorlas as they emerge.

The figures lack the artistic subtlety of using terracotta or other coloured tesserae in their outlines to soften and provide an element of solidity and dimension to their forms, as is most often found on figured mosaics. The hair of the telamones is formed by intersecting arcs of blue tesserae, and they have red nipples and navels. Their white skin has somewhat crude joint and muscle lines and no genitals, which the mosaicist seems not to have considered necessary on any of the pavement's naked figures. Lack of genitalia occurs elsewhere on other Romano-British mosaics such as at Horkstow, North Lincolnshire, and Lenthay Green, Dorset and is not significant. The technique used on these figures replicates in 'positive' the 'negative' depictions so often encountered in Roman mosaic, namely, black figures with white anatomical detailing as survive at many Roman sites such as at Ostia Antica, near Rome, and in the upper gallery of the Baths of Caracalla in Rome itself.

Telamones on mosaic are incredibly rare and these walking versions are seemingly only matched by four on a restored mosaic in the Greek Cross Hall at the Vatican, found at Tusculum in 1741. This combination of telamones and mandorlas appears to be unique in floor mosaic. To discover examples in Berkshire is

A model of the temple of the Olympian Zeus showing the placement of the colossal telamones. (AB)

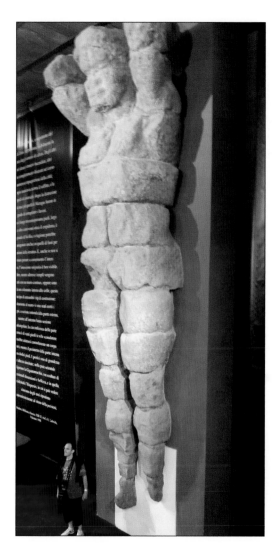

A telamon from the temple of the Olympian Zeus at Agrigento museum. (AB)

quite remarkable. The figures predate those of Christ stepping from an oval blue mandorla that appear in early Christian art. Two of Boxford's telamones retain most of their features, the northern one being beautifully intact. The corner placement of the telamones reminds one of a battered but rather fine 2nd or 3rd century AD example of a garden fountain from Avenches and now in the Musée Romains d'Avenches. This fountain features four abraded corner telamones supporting the roof of a structure that perhaps represents a garden pavilion but once had the practical function of being the fountain's reservoir.

The inspiration for telamones is unknown, although the connection with Atlas holding up the sky seems highly likely. The Roman architect Vitruvius says of them: "Again, figures in the form of men supporting mutules or coronae, we term 'telamones' – the reasons why or wherefore they are so called are not found in any story – but the Greeks call them 'atlantes'. For Atlas is described in story as holding up the firmament because, through his vigorous intelligence and ingenuity, he was the first to cause men to be taught about the courses of the sun and moon, and the laws governing the revolutions of all the constellations. Consequently, in recognition of this benefaction, painters and sculptors represent him as holding up the firmament, and the atlantides, his daughters, whom we call 'Vergiliae' and the Greeks 'Pleiades', are consecrated in the firmament among the constellations." (Vitruvius, The Ten Books on Architecture. Book vi, chapter vii, 6.)

The south-east telamon was the first part of the mosaic uncovered in 2017 to hint at the singularity of the mosaic. (AB)

The earliest architectural telamones known in the classical world are those colossal 8 metre high statues that ornamented the largest Doric-style temple of antiquity, the Olympieion or Temple of Zeus at Akragas (now Agrigento) on Sicily. Dating to around 480-470 BC, these Atlas-type male figures acted as semi-engaged pilasters situated below the architrave and between engaged Doric columns. With their hands raised behind their heads, they seemingly bore the weight of the colossal structure's roof. Their striking appearance was to inspire imitation in other forms of Sicilian art and telamones would later appear to have become almost emblematic of ancient Sicily. The idea of stone and terracotta human figures in the

The north-east telamon is the most damaged and also lost its feet to the land drain. (AB)

The south-west telamon fortunately retains half of its face. The combination of the dark blue mandorlas with telamones seems unique. (AB)

form of engaged columns would spread from the Greek kingdoms of Sicily to find popularity throughout the Greek, Etruscan and Roman worlds. The use of telamones at Boxford may refer to Atlas being the father of Sterope and the rumoured sire of Pelops.

The Triumphal Amorini

In the centre of the border on each side of the mosaic are blue-backed guilloche bordered roundels out of which leap *amorini* (winged cupids). When the first was uncovered in 2017, it was expected that these would represent the seasons as are commonly found on mosaics and it was thought that the eastern one held a wreath of flowers representing Spring. As mentioned above, the seasons are often found in association with Bellerophon mosaics as Pegasus and Bellerophon form the impetus to set the year rolling. However upon excavation it was found that all bore the same attribute of a wreath in their left hands. Only part of the border of the southern roundel now remains but the others are mostly intact. They are naked but are backed by red sashes that are not attached around the waist as usually occurs. The usual red nipples and navels are evident and their oddly drawn muscles give them remarkably smiling torsos so much so that the eastern one received the name of 'Happy

Left: The north-west telamon remains in beautiful condition and seems to have been the most accomplished. (AB)

The western roundel is the finest and has a traditionally classical feel. Unlike the others, it holds a linchpin as a connection with the chariot race behind it. (AB)

Tummy'. Their wings rather resemble flags in shape.

The finest amorino incorporating tiny tesserae and with its head in a classically tilted pose is that on the western side below the chariot race. It has a sensitive face and its right hand clasps a linchpin through the loop, in reference to the panel above. This is the only one holding something in its right hand. It has been suggested to me that all are about to fight with buckler and sword but this was generally a medieval contest (although a gladiator does appear with a small round shield on the tomb of C Lusius Storax at Chieti Museum dating from around 30 BC). Apart from the eastern amorino, the others are holding red quoit-like wreaths and their white hands appear at the centre of each. The eastern amorino has this reversed, whether by mistake or intention is unknown. Given the triumphal theme of the mosaic it seems more likely that they are each holding golden victory wreaths, the Corona Triumphalis. A good example appears on the Byzantine ivory Veroli casket in the Victoria and Albert Museum where Bellerophon's taming of Pegasus is celebrated by an amorino in almost the exact pose wielding just such a wreath above his head. Such a crown of victory appears above Pelops on the Cumae sarcophagus.

The northern roundel's amorino has yellow hair, and the usual white wings and red sash. (AB)

Hercules and the Centaur

The Hercules group occupies the southern half of the east border. Although rarely encountered on Roman mosaics in Britain, the hero Hercules (Heracles to the Greeks) does occur widely in all other forms of Romano-British decorative art. The Hercules and centaur mosaic group is the first British example of this scene, based originally on a lost (but once famous) sculpture. Mosaics showing all or some of the twelve labours of Hercules occur throughout the Roman Empire but thus far none have been discovered in Britain beyond a mosaic at Bramdean, in Hampshire, of Hercules and Antaeus, a story attached to the eleventh labour. The Boxford Hercules shows another episode attached to a labour.

The Myths

Hercules was the child of an unwitting liason between Zeus (Jupiter) and the mortal Alcmene, when the king of the gods took the form of her husband to seduce her. In some accounts she was the granddaughter of Pelops and Hippodamia which links Hercules to the hero. Humiliated by her husband's behaviour, Hera (Juno), the queen of the gods, bore a hatred towards the hero throughout his life. Driven insane by her, Hercules slew his son, daughter, and wife Megara. When restored to sanity, the horrified hero sought redemption from the Oracle of Delphi. He

Opposite: The Hercules and centaur group of the eastern border. (AB)

was advised to serve his cousin King Eurystheus of Tiryns for twelve years, performing whatever labours were set him.

Whilst engaged on his fourth labour (the quest to capture the fearsome Erymanthian boar), Hercules rested at the cave of his kindly centaur friend Pholus. The latter fed Hercules but refused his request for wine because the amphora was a communal one owned by all the centaurs. Regardless of this, Hercules broke the vessel open to drink. The smell of the wine drew all the neighbouring centaurs to the house where, enraged by his actions, they forcibly entered armed with stones and tree branches. Hercules attacked them, killing many with his club and then shooting others with arrows, and it is likely that this is the episode commemorated here.

More famously, Hercules also killed the centaur Nessus for the attempted violation of his wife Deianira after he had ferried her across the river Evenus. In that case Hercules used a poisoned arrow rather than a club although on the great mosaic from Saint-Leu (Portus Magnus), Algeria (known as 'La Grande Mosaique des Luttes') he adopts a similar stretched pose to Boxford's but with his knee on the centaur's back and the club in his hand. A cupid additionally stabs the dying centaur with a spear or large arrow. Saint-Leu's group is placed in a river (the Evenus) whose deity appears at the right of the panel

_____

Opposite: A detail of the centaur's head. His arm adopts the fatal pose grasping his assailant's hand and showing that he is doomed. (AB)

so that, at least, must represent the death of Nessus. Yet a third centaur killed by Hercules was Eurytion who was slain because he was forcing Mnesimache to marry him during the fifth labour (cleaning the stables of Augeus at Pelops' old kingdom of Elis). Hercules is credited with having established the violent boxing and wrestling contest called the pancratium at Olympia in honour of his ancestor Pelops.

The Mosaic – Hercules in action

Although depicted as a simple line drawing, the mosaicist has endowed the group with great energy. The figure of Hercules lunges forward, adopting a classic and vibrant pose of conflict often encountered in Greco-Roman art. The perspective and modelling of his thighs and legs is well handled and only spoiled by the position of his right foot. His figure steps out of the panel's surrounding blue fillet and stands upon the red border. Hercules raises his right arm behind his head to deal the death blow with his club that is solidly portrayed in grey tesserae. Although the lower part of his face is now destroyed, his eyes survive, looking towards the centaur's torso. Like those of the telamones, his abdominal muscles are stylised into two blue elongated circles, and the joints and calf muscles are also indicated. Red tesserae mark his nipples and navel, but again the mosaicist has not considered it important to depict genitals. From his right shoulder, the famous Nemean lion skin streams out, indicating the violent motion of the hero.

The drawing of the centaur is less fluid than that of

Hercules but is, notwithstanding, well handled. Like his aggressor, his hair is formed by overlapping arcs of blue tesserae on the white field. He leans backwards and the powerful muscles of his torso, his 'six-pack', are indicated and stressed by blue lines. Again, red tesserae indicate his nipples and navel.

A shaggy fur cloak of grey tesserae layered by lines of blue streams out from his left side as he turns. It is decorated with a fashionable *orbiculus* or 'roundel'. In his right hand he holds a rock, one of the traditional weapons used by centaurs. Below it his tail flows away and curls between Hercules' legs. The hero grabs his victim by the hair whilst the centaur's left arm bends backwards and his hand comes to rest on the victor's wrist. This is the 'fatal pose', used in classical art to indicate to the viewer that the victim is doomed and death imminent. The unbearded centaur here is dragged backwards and his front legs bow outwards and stray beyond the blue border fillet. The two tesserae that form his mouth afford him a remarkably calm and gentle expression as he looks towards his slayer. Currently, the closest parallel to the Boxford group occurs on a side panel of the late-2nd century AD Hercules sarcophagus, once in the Astor collection at Hever Castle, Kent. The popularity of this image continued and is found on a 5th century AD Hercules *contorniate* (medallion) issued during the reign of Valentinian III.

The Cantharus

To the right of the triumphal cupid sits a *cantharus* or wine cup. It is wide mouthed and has elaborate tendril handles and gadrooning. Framed by bushes, it appears to be simply a garden ornament and alluding to Bacchus and the pleasures of wine and, until the panel below was properly understood, this is how it was interpreted. As the excavation continued in 2019 it seemed a strange decoration for borders so filled with action and incident. However its symbolism and placing in the border is very subtle as it sits directly above the head of the enthroned figure of Oenomaus in the court panel below it. Oenomaus' name translates as 'man of wine' so its presence cleverly confirms the identification of the subject on the throne in the viewer's mind. Subtleties such as this convince one that the decorative scheme of this mosaic was carefully planned. Possibly the owner's chair was placed here on the eastern coarse border facing this.

Opposite: The cantharus or wine cup of the eastern border above the image of the enthroned Oenomaus 'man of wine'. It was designed to be seen from the coarse border, and possibly this was the view from the owner's chair. Visitors would have viewed him above the 'court panel'. (AB)

Alcathous of Elis and the Cithaeronian Lion

At the north-eastern corner, a Victorian land drain cut through the tessellated border of the mosaic but caused very little damage and provides a cross-section of its foundation. Here the mosaic border has gently subsided into a filled pit that preceded it. Apart from bushes, the triumphal cupid and the telamones, the only figure found in the northern border is a delightful one of an archer. The importance of this figure in British mosaics cannot be overstressed as uniquely it connects with a figure in the western border. Such a connection of action between separate borders is certainly unique in British mosaics and an extreme rarity if occurring elsewhere in the empire. The idea seems based on the sort of decoration one might find in the borders of illuminated manuscripts. The action adds to the three-dimensional effect attempted by the mosaicist as the archer fires an arrow *behind* the back of the north-western telamon and into the throat of a fleeing lion in the western border. This beautifully preserved north-western corner proved to be the favourite area of the mosaic with its excavators.

The archer is dressed in a fashionable 4th century AD tunic complete with orbiculi at the shoulder and thigh and a clavus stripe at the side of the neck. Bands decorate the tunic at the wrists. On his shoulder he wears a red chlamys (cloak) that streams behind him and his feet are clad in cross-laced hunting boots called cothurni. He pulls a recurved and composite bow, the standard weapon of Roman imperial archers, which breaks into and disrupts the flow of the guilloche border surrounding the central panels. The target of the hunter's arrow is a perfectly preserved fleeing lion in the western border. Similar in design to the lion-headed Chimaera and illustrative of the lost areas of that figure, the animal turns to snarl at his tormentor as an arrow enters his throat and blood spurts forth. He is provided with a large red tongue and splendidly sharp teeth.

The Myth

The Boxford archer may perhaps be identified with Alcathous of Elis, the son of Pelops and Hippodamia, and the lion with that of Cithaeron. When Prince Euippus of Megara was killed by a terrifying lion on Mount Cithaeron, his father King Megareus offered his kingdom and the hand of his daughter Euaechme to whoever could slay the animal. Alcathous undertook the task, slew the lion and won the prize. In grateful thanks he built a temple to Apollo the Hunter and Artemis the Huntress at Megara that was still standing in the 2nd century AD when the Greek traveller and author Pausanius visited it and recorded the story of the lion in his *Description of Greece*.

Opposite: Alcathous with a composite bow and hunting boots. (AB)

Arion and Adrastus

The final group in the western border is the most enigmatic on the mosaic both for its subject matter and also its execution. It is damaged but apparently depicts a young man (or huntress) dressed in a knee-length red, white and blue striped tunic moving towards a horse. That he is dressed suggests that he is mortal. At first glance he appears to be holding a grey sceptre, staff or spear but the object is held at its extremity in his raised left hand so is unlikely to be a weapon. Unfortunately, a large section of the lower figure is lost and with it the end of the object, and what remains of the border has leaves, a stem and one isolated blue tessera remaining. His right hand exists and is clasping something although large-leaved foliage also seems to be growing through or behind it and also in the area around his head. The horse has lost most of its neck and the top of its raised left leg. He is unbridled and that may be a clue to the action. The figure appears to be about to tether the horse with the object which presumably curved around either to his other hand or to the horse's neck. The animal is naively drawn and executed and, although following the technique used on the other horses, is obviously not by the same mosaicist. In startling contrast to this is the figure of the youth, which for some reason uses the smallest tesserae found anywhere on the floor (and

Opposite: A detail of the lion struck by Alcathous' arrow. (AB)

possibly in Britain) on his arms as some are less than 2mm square.

The Myths

When first uncovered, the author wondered if this part of the mosaic portrayed the episode when the young Alexander the Great tethered and tamed the stallion Bucephalus by realising that the animal was frightened of its own shadow. However, as it became clear that all the other motifs in the borders have some allusion to either Pelops or Poseidon a new candidate was needed. One might be the youth Hippothous, son of Poseidon and Alope (daughter of King Cercyon of Eleusis), who was exposed out of shame by his mother but suckled by a mare before being rescued by shepherds. When the king subsequently discovered the birth, the boy was again exposed and once more suckled by the mare. The shepherds then named him Hippothous ('impetuous stallion'). After killing Cercyon, Theseus made him king of Eleusis.

However, probably the most likely candidates are the divine stallion Arion and Adrastus, his third owner. Poseidon had wanted to have sex with Demeter (Ceres) and she, still searching for her abducted daughter and in order to avoid his attentions, changed herself into a mare and mingled with the horses owned by Oncius (or Oncus) a son of Apollo and king of Onceium, a region of Arcadia. Poseidon, however, changed himself into a stallion and covered her. The result was a fabulous horse called Arion ('moon creature on high') who was raised

Arion and Adrastus. (AB)

A reconstruction of Arion and Adrastus. (AB)

by the sea nymphs and also pulled Poseidon's chariot 'with uncommon swiftness'. He was half-brother again to Bellerophon and Pegasus. Poseidon gave Arion to Oncius who later gave him to Hercules as the latter was starting a military campaign against Elis. Preferring to fight on foot he later gave him to Adrastus, king of Argos, who won the prize at the Nemean Games on him. He became known as the Horse of Adrastus, and Pausanius remarked that Antimachus had said of Arion: "Adrastus was the third lord who tamed him." (Pausanias, Description of Greece 8.25.10). The author's suggestion is that Adrastus is shown taming Arion and about to tether or bridle him. The group bares a remarkable similarity to a famous 3rd century BC southern Italian tomb painting from Egnazia known as 'The Horse or Foal Tamer'. Apart from speed, Arion was also credited with the remarkable powers of speech and flight. Adrastus was later saved by Arion when he fled from the disastrous campaign known as The Seven Against Thebes.

Materials and the Mosaicists

It is often assumed that mosaicists used locally found materials for their commissions but this was certainly not the case at Boxford. The tesserae used in the floor have been identified by buildings material specialist Dr Kevin Hayward as dark blue-grey and buff-grey dolostone from the Upper Jurassic beds at Kimmeridge Bay or from an adjacent outcrop along the Dorset coast. Similar tesserae from the same source appear at Silchester. Brownstone tesserae were also identified. This Devonian brownstone originates from The Forest of Dean and was used for mosaics at both Silchester and at the Groundwell Ridge complex near Swindon. The white tesserae are indurated (hardened) chalk from the Upper Cretaceous beds originating possibly from the Dorset or Hampshire Downs and also white Lias, a fine white limestone from the Triassic beds of Somerset. Red is terracotta building material and used both in the coarse border and the main pavement. According to Kevin Hayward a similar suite of materials occurred at the villa at Dinnington in Somerset. It leads one to question whether the mosaicists themselves originated in Dorset bringing the materials with them, or if there was a manufacturing supplier of ready-made mosaic tesserae sticks, based at one of the quarries in the Kimmeridge area of the county. Where pink tesserae occur in some areas of the mosaic these are of chalk that has been altered by heat. Interestingly pink tesserae seem to have been chosen for one of the horses so the use there is intentional. In laying the pavement, the tesserae were grouted and sat on a thin layer of lime-bonding cement. Below was a compact reddish sand about 3cm thick then below that a compact chalk and light brown silty clay including some mortar fragments and small rounded pebble inclusions. This latter deposit was of unknown depth. The chalk must have come from a nearby chalk pit as the site geology is clay.

CONCLUSION

The Boxford mosaic is arguably the most important example of late Roman art to have been discovered in Britain. Its importance lies not in the technical or artistic abilities of the mosaicists who made it but in the remarkable choice of subjects depicted, the innovative approach of the mosaicists and their attempts to produce a trompe l'oeil design. The choice of images, all seemingly subtly connected to Pelops, Bellerophon or Poseidon are of great interest and originality in art and must surely have been chosen with care by the patron. The aristocratic horse theme is strong with six being portrayed on the floor and also so pertinent for the Vale of Lambourn, the modern 'valley of the racehorse' especially as Poseidon claimed to have invented horse racing! Indeed the supposition amongst the excavators was that this might have been a stud or a hunting lodge.

The inscriptions in themselves are very unusual for Britain, and give us names of the main characters featured and the possible owners' names. Only on the mosaic at Thruxton do we have owners' names although one may have featured at Hawkesbury and be hidden in the inscription at Lullingstone. The apparent childlike naivety of the figures should be viewed keeping what little we know of contemporary manuscript illumination in mind. Indeed the 5th century *Virgilius Romanus*, in the Vatican, believed by many to be a Romano-British manuscript, has a great similarity in the naivety of its figures. It may well be that the mosaic's patron requested the panels to be copied from a favourite manuscript in his collection. We know that the story of Pelops was covered in the works of Sophocles, Euripides, Accius and Pherecydes to name but a few and other works such as *The Fabulae of Hyginus* or *Apollodorus' Library* may have provided inspiration. Certainly the lively borders suggest this. The similarity with some aspects of the Pelops panel at Noheda also suggests that both mosaics are based on a once-famous original. This also raises questions as to the singular spelling of Bellerefons' that is only known from the Malaga mosaic. Is there an Iberian connection either with the mosaic's designer, patron or mosaicist? Comparison with the Noheda Pelops mosaic and sarcophagi featuring the story shows that Boxford's version follows a recognised artistic tradition in combining a tableau at the court of Oenomaus together with the major composition of the race.

The work of the Boxford mosaicist has, thus far, not been identified elsewhere in Britain but that does not mean that he was from another province of the Empire. Differences in the treatment of such things as hands and eyes suggest that two or possibly three mosaicists worked on the pavement. One gives his figures distinctively stump-like hands with one or two fingers. Interestingly, the Croughton Bellerophon mosaic seemingly does retain simplified elements of the figurework at Boxford but at a far remove and may be a later work by the least talented of the craftsmen, or another mosaicist using the same cartoon. The design of the hero's face with its rectangular nose brings to mind those of Boxford, whereas elements of Croughton's Pegasus – the mane, eye and musculature – also have echoes of the treatment of horses here, especially on the figure of Arion. However, Croughton's tail composed of a single line of tesserae is a poor substitute for Boxford's splendid tails.

Unquestionably one of the most notable and apparent eccentricities of Boxford's mosaic is the fact that figures are not contained by their borders but overlap or break out of them. This overlapping is similar to that sometimes encountered in sculptural friezes and in late Roman manuscript illumination. It is worth noting that the *Virgilius Romanus'* famous illumination showing Dido and Aeneas sheltering from a downpour in a cave has a guard sitting above their refuge whose spear pierces the borders, bringing to mind the armed man in the court panel. This overlapping occurs with other items on more pages of the manuscript. Indeed, by the 5th century one also frequently finds the same overlapping of borders by figures and objects carved on the ivory diptychs that once ornamented the covers of codices. So it may well be that in their apparent disregard for the sanctity of borders, the mosaicists at Boxford were actually following a modern fashion found in other artistic media but not yet recognised in British mosaics. It is perhaps another clue to linking the inspiration for the Boxford mosaics to a *codex* (book) possibly owned by the patron. The similarities of draughtsmanship and overlap with aspects of late antique manuscript illumination and ivory diptych panels such as the 5th century AD Bellerophon panel in the British Museum (inventory no. 1856.6-23.2) must raise the possibility that such a source was the inspiration for the mosaicists. Naive and untidy in its design the mosaic certainly is, but it possesses a great magic that entranced all who excavated it, as it no doubt did Caepio and Fortunata in the 4th century AD.

The Roman visitor entering from the southern door and viewing the mosaic would have been confronted by the image of Bellerophon and a riot of other decoration. (AB)